Empty as Nirvana

Audio Collections by Zayra Yves

Crowned Compassion
Sleep in the Sea Tonight with Me

Empty as Nirvana

Zayra Yves

Empty as Nirvana
Copyright © 2007 by Zayra Yves

Contact the author: **www.zayrayves.com**

Front Cover Photograph: Angelo Cavalli
Cover Design: Brian Douthit

ISBN: 978-0-6151-5123-6

Magdalena & Co.
Santa Clara, CA

Only from the heart can you touch the sky.
Rumi

Acknowledgements:

Some of the poems in *Empty as Nirvana* appear in a slightly different form from their original publication. Changes made by the author are in this edition. The author wishes to thank the editors and DJ's of the following publications or radio shows where some of the poems in *Empty as Nirvana* were previously published or released by audio: *The Zimbabwe Situation; The Panhandler Quarterly; Voices for Africa; Eyes of the Poet; Reflections IIT Madras (India); Edge Life Magazine, Poetry Life & Times; Astropoetica; Alehouse Press; Kreativ; House of the Poet; Integral Naked; TWiN; Perfectly Said; SW Radio Africa, Mazunge Studio One and Zenzala; Coolfire (United Kingdom).*

The author would like to thank Brian Douthit for all of his amazing support and generous spirit in helping to create this book, as well as for promoting it to audiences at large. She offers gratitude and love to Eric Galpine for countless hours of sacrifice, faith and support. She also has deep appreciation for the following people: Antonio Araujo, Dominic Angerame, Audrey & Stuart, Mike Begbie, Nagi Chami, Dana Coulston, Stewart Cubley, Corey de Vos, Richard Dorian, Jim Dunlap, Michael Hannon, Chris Hudson, Tererai Karimakwenda, Em'Kal, Myra Lochner, Losa, Neil Ludwig, Saurabh Madaan, Joan McKee, Mondoro, Credo Mutwa, Michael Nichols, Margo Perin, Ron, Stefano Resta, Barbara Sawicki, Saidi Semakula, Tom Spearman, Leslie Sundt, Mike Thomas, Linda Tucker, the White Lions and Nicolette van der Walt for all of their contributions toward promoting or supporting the works that appear in this book, as well as in the audio collections. She is deeply grateful to her friends and family for their commitment to the arts, as well as their continued support to living life from the heart in solidarity, truth and compassionate spirit.

A portion of the proceeds from this book will be donated to: www.shareyoursoles.org

In Loving Memory of Al Robins

Contents:

I.   Returning to the Garden

II.   Clear as Blue

III. Bone Fragments

IV. Salt in the Heartland

V. Sky Rivers

"A real flower comes in the morning, laughs for a moment, spreads its fragrance and is gone."

Osho

Foreword

Zayra Yves is a true artist; a being of light conveying our collective experiences within temporal reality; a beautiful woman sharing her spirit-expressions while still dancing in and out of this world of duality; a passion-filled force embracing both her human vulnerabilities as well as the divine essence.

In this book, Zayra Yves takes us on a journey that begins deep within her own wonderful heart and expands outward over the earth to eventually comprise the universe itself. Divided into five sections, *Empty as Nirvana* is a unique blend of a life lived with profound sincerity along with the maturity of an experienced writer. *Returning to the Garden* is a more personal glimpse into Zayra's existence surrounded by love, in the physical as well as the spiritual. She has the ability to paint with words utterly delightful images overflowing with arousal and serenity as in these lines from, "In Praise Of Your Body":

You emerge from a pale sea
and your limbs invite the names of flowers:
jasmine, rose and tiger lily...
I see the colors of poppies and dandy lion,
the juice of cantaloupe.

Clear as Blue and *Bone Fragments* are both a glances backward. The former is a testament of how love can touch our lives with people and events we hope to always remember, with the latter being a more acrid view.

In *Salt in the Heartland*, Zayra shows us equally the blinding beauty and distressing tragedies that can be found on the continent of Africa. Due to a lack of any natural resource and real economic influence, many in the international community view Africa as being of no real consequence or importance. Zayra reminds us that the real resource in Africa can be found within the warmth and nobility of its people. Originally a contest-winning composition, and subsequently released on her audio CD *Crowned Compassion*, she has included her much celebrated poem, "Free Us From The Claws Of Cruelty" in this book, and I point to a small excerpt here:

Walk with me into the heritage of ruins,
through gateways built by ancient tribes,
and listen as they speak on the dry wind
with incantations.

Oh, Great Spirits, this is a land of ancestors
where once women ruled as queens and lovers
and the white lion was free.

So, tell me how it is that our own torture us -
take children for slaves, turn blood against blood,
burn farms, deprive of us care...

Zayra wrote this moving poem specifically for the inhabitants of Zimbabwe after traveling there. She eloquently conveys the absolute dignity of the past and the current strife of the present. This poem brilliantly leaves the reader somewhere on the edge of hope and perhaps even praying for some miracle, just as the wonderful people of Zimbabwe might.

Conceivably an allusion to the Milky Way, *Sky Rivers* includes her poems containing stars, the heavens, and the cosmos. Not only in this section, but throughout the book, Zayra maintains her high vision of human existence. She whispers us mysteries and presents to us sparkling jewels that shimmer with life and love. She is a welcome and comforting voice to all of us souls who occupy this world with her.

Brian Douthit - Author, Editor, Reviewer

Returning to the Garden

Speak to Me of Flowers

Let me swallow your words.
I will ask nothing else but to live
on the dust of your pollen.

Benediction

A string of prayer flags
folded into rectangles
imperfect squares
tied together
and written in ten languages,
stained the color of truth
with words I might have said
but didn't
now rolled into a cloth scroll
I have packed and unpacked
several times over
in strange rooms
on unfamiliar streets
with swinging lanterns
and closed faces in the alley
smoking desert cigarettes
lit in the night
as I have wandered
by camel caravan,
elephant, and horse
as I have traveled by plane
by boat and by trains
across continents, sand dunes
over the waters
and back again
listening for your name
that I might discover
you there.

Crowned Compassion

I rise on this plateau from another world,
from the world beyond, from the roots of virtue
and noble intention. I rise from a prayer
part land, part stone, part divine imagination and clay.

I am carved from the human life here in this world,
from hands that have known sorrow, innocence, loss;
from hands that have known drunkenness and love-lust.

I am formed simultaneous as all movement, motion, aware.
Born as a Bodhisattva, as a friend, as the Eternal Mother;
as the embodiment of attributes both strong and slender.

I grow from the roots of non-attachment as Bodhicitta,
as the relief from torment and suffering I grow up
out of the dirt, mud, rock toward the sun, rain, sky.

I evolve as porcelain insight, blue as the universe
unfolding brilliant white, glowing constellation
star by star, blossoming consciousness petal by petal,
crystal as the lotus from the pure land I emerge.

Divine Muse

Your soul rises from the mantra
of sacred sound:

a universe of patchouli, rosemary, ginger
and lantern blue.

Your feet painted with small trees
and petite lyrics

in vines of sorrow and remembering
that spin up your legs.

Your hips covered with nubile promise
in a tiny garden:

peach, mango and passion fruit
that blossom inside your skin

as flowers under the expanse of sky
painted on your torso to breasts of fire.

You are no longer the aesthetic image,
as your sweet throat invites the poet

to taste the flavor drawn on your lips
that only open when kissed.

Longing is an Echo Shrill Inside

Your ghost howls then bends
Arches indigo through the tunnel
To bring on this event

Never mind the rain
Pouring a monsoon down my face
Or chasing the metro

I wait in this steel shelter
Man made and smelling of gray
Slipping on wet cement

Listening for your voice
To erase memory

I carve a totem from my insides
Asymmetrical of balsa wood and stones

It is the not knowing
That has brought me here
Tight and loose as a bouquet

You too may desire unity
Hope for a moveable feast

Let me embrace you
Even as I am

Transgressed in silk, my seasonal trinkets
Birthing turtles, eating moon cakes
Holding grasshoppers in my bag

Appear as you are

A line of body eclipsing the light
Speaking the language of our instincts
Ineffable, immortal, teaming with lions

Trim your absence with ardent feelings
I await who knows what inclinations
In the daylight, clutched at the breast

I WANT YOU

I want you sweet as cinnamon, warm as butter on toast.

I want you in me soft, flickering as a candle flame.

I want you deep blue, abstract and painted in flowers.

I want you as a prayer written a thousand times, tucked in a pillow.

I want you aging, ripening on the vine, as pure as Burgundy,
as Merlot.

I want you as a song five times a day in a hundred countries.

I want you as a risk, as a skydiver dives off a cliff.

I want you as a wish, as lyrical, as loyal as dolphins swim.

I want you loose as spilled milk, dripping down the sides.

I want you in me zipped as a twin, tight as a reason.

I want you midnight fragrant as African air, as distant.

I want you to play me as a harp, harmonica, flute or guitar.

I want you intoxicated dancing bare on a cloud in the rain.

I want you bright orange, hot as mouth blown glass.

I want you as a vixen, slut, love machine.

I want you as a saint, Mother Mary, Jesus, and Allah too.

I want you wrapped around my skin as a blanket on Christmas.

I want you sleeping curled under the covers faithful as a dog.

I want you aloof as a cat lounging on the windowsill.

I want you wise as an owl, royal as an eagle, free as a falcon.

I want you laughing, bubbling over, sparkling as champagne.

I want you as a mystery, a story, as someone I may have imagined.

I want you dressed, undressed, clothes over the chair, on the floor.

I want your name revealed in my world as someone eternal.

I want you naked, raw, exposed as an oyster on the half shell.

I want you to crawl out of my dreams to join me.

I want you here, now.

Our Passions Might be Numbered Like This

One:

this morning cherry blossoms fall from the garden tree
kiss my arm soundlessly, pale light, and drift away
from my skin, like your eyelashes folded in sleep
belonging to no one, not silence, not me

Two:

open your mouth, open it now, feel my finger
as I trace the rim of your lips moist plum
feel my tongue as I kiss the rim of your ear
the shell of the s curve circling around the center

Three:

it only hurts where you do not touch me, rising
in half as split kiwi exposing the tiny seeds of wonder
I show you how morning glory opens in pink dawn
mindless as a body waiting for the heat of day to arrive

Four:

let us walk naked away from the onyx shores
side by side shedding our hair, nails and teeth
in the cyan waters of surplus where clumsy things swim
graceful, blind, without remiss, bubbles escape from lips

Five:

into the palms of your hands the arch of my feet fit
where you become the water reshaping faces of rocks
as I curve into your arm, torso, belly button and heat
like a mountain caving into a basin without names

Six:

ours is without deliberation as the dam gives way
to rivers and streams flushing in a slow moan,
a long sigh from the throat in a shadow city
where red tongues lick olive oil and basil

Seven:

in mid sentence under a hanging branch with chimes
honey mango and ripe where your body meets mine
this slender pelvis kiss, because a kiss is just a kiss
do not blame me for being positioned like this

In Praise of Your Body

It is more than parted skin or open mouths.
It is more than a song hidden in the bone.

You emerge from a pale sea
and your limbs invite the names of flowers:
jasmine, rose and tiger lily.
I see the colors of poppies and dandy lion,
the juice of cantaloupe.

You appear earthen as terracotta
bright as a sunflower field,
spacious and luminous
as if you swallowed the seed of love
to keep it alive.

Plum Blossoms

ten thousand petals deep
each one floating as a lifetime

in the art of falling
no different from stars
dancing out of blackness

predestined to be more
yet, uncertain

in the weightless air
of what cannot be seen

here: just bury me

in the shadow of dreams
beneath the last blossom
            as it fell

Returning to the Garden

Come as you are, I will take you into my body. This living temple that nourished you with blood, bone and soul. I will welcome you into the inner most sanctuary and nourish you in the soil, in the cathedral of my flesh, in primal eternity. You, my precious one, born from chaos, from the waters of silence, from the wisdom of light, from basalt, granite. I will swallow the flame, have you unchained and free to dance as a lover, as the one who spins night and day on her axis. Fall like rain into my arms as you slip from the silver gray of skin into the petal silk of an orchid suspended in time. I will open gateways to celestial bodies beyond anything your mind imagines, so you will remember this love you were born for. My hands will free you from the ruins, heal scars, raise you up from extinct; as you return again to incarnate full of desire and double helix. I will embrace you weighing more than water, less than light, as you go in search of death, as your ashes scatter in the winds. Between the borders of enemy, of friend, we will meet. I will cherish you as the incantation, the shadow and the cry of life. Come as you are, enter the river of my eyes speaking the language of fire, of dreams, unfolding body into body, joining us in love again.

Butterfly Verse

one more hour
      of daylight
and if you speak the words
that shine with approval

silently I might drift
into a cloud -

move stiff wings
off the pages of anthologies
      flee the dragon's fire

      to land
luminous as a glint of silk
on your open hand

Shaman's Love Song

On the wild breath of the open wind
I call you with my heart.

Listen to me as I translate love,
as I forge a prayer from your body
that is hard like a sad stone.

Your body without a dream.

Feel my heart as it rushes like rivers
bringing to you all things both seen and
un-manifest, both living and dying and
being born again.

Let your body soften into mine like clay.

Feel my heart as it dances on fire,
as it embraces your diverse
and precarious nature.

Let your love blossom, quench your thirst
and drink from this heart of mine
as lions drink from the still waters of time.

My soul is the imagination you hunted
in the desires of your desire.

My love will remove the poison of resentment,
of pride; of those who did not intend to hurt you,
but did not love you either.

This love will erase bitter memories
from the cracked rocks
in the mountains of your mind.

And we will have all naked night to swim
in the lapis sea of my body.

Reach out to me with your renegade soul
and I will make a bed of flowers
for your orphaned spirit.

Where you will feel sublime,
full of grace and courage.

I call to you from the waters of dreams
where you will find solace in my embrace;
where prayers from the rainmaker bring rain.

Feel your heart as it leaves gravity
        to fly with life again.

Feel this love as an answer, as true and real
waiting for you to open;
waiting for you to see I am the one.

Listen to me as I translate love,
as I forge a prayer from your body,
that is hard like a sad stone.

Your body without a dream...just say "Yes."

Clear as Blue

Gathering Light in a Bottle

The color blue still reminds me of you.

A night in Egypt cannot cure it.
Neither the scent of yellow curry
or women draped in saris of gold.

Magical stories, courier pigeons
or breaking the bread of grace,
cannot cure it.

Fleshy bodies, flowers spurting
through craggy rocks, walks
in the dark.

Nothing cures me of images,
like the way you hold your spoon,
or the risks of sitting on clouds.

Postcards of color fill a cigar box
I never intended to take with me
as a ghost of love.

But I have. Worse than that
I have written pieces of words,
fragments really

of our conversations no bigger
than recipes, no smaller
than entries.

I do not mourn you anymore
or feel you, except the pictures
of us on the sea floor;

except the bare arm closing
the shower door just after a kiss
or slender foot of mint.

Random I purchase petite things
I cannot become attached to
or that won't take long

to pack: lavender soap, stamps,
bangles, crystals, door knobs and
rings...

little glass bottles empty as nirvana
in the center of a window
soaking up the light.

Evaporation

Surrounded by the deep rush
of waves, we made love.
I knew enlightenment would never last.

It was all a lie
this idea of nirvana and lotus
cherry pose of tantra
as your tongue entered
my mouth.

I could feel you were thirsty
for every last drop.
And, I gave myself to you
orbiting in shadows
as our bodies curved into rings
faster than light.

We could not quench our thirst
for licking moisture
between shoulder blades,
for sucking between legs
and kissing ankles.

We drank our words,
swallowed whole names in moans
and we did not stop
until we collapsed into salt.

Gravity of Love

The stone that was your heart
fell out of your chest while we made love.
It dropped into mine with a muffled song
that an orca might call their own.

Small and round, I carry you in me
feeling the echo more than I hear it.

And, when I wish to hold you, I cannot.

The weight and gravity of love falling
into the depths of me, ripples
and ripples in silence.

Extracts of a Beached Love Story

In a cloud of cynicism
and rusted joints,
you pontificate about poor Love
interrogated daily,
and boast of the skylark
now plucked clean;
stark dead
in white silence.

Laugh as the heart is dismembered
like the body of Osiris...
thrown to dogs,
buried under trees,
collected for jars.

I remember you
before your mind was cut
on a transgressive shell
and bled into the sea.

Your flags of loyalty
abandoned like songs
between the brothel and church
of spiritual shipwreck.

No angels were there
for your shameless plenitudes
of generous genius,
or for the death of a madman
and our lady of the streets.

Love, like a skeleton
washed up on the shore,
infested with symptoms,
no more than useless arguments,
as if she were the product of
a good screw, the zodiac
and ironic.

You cannot redress your words
or hear my heart
skip a beat.

Saudade

You said it was easy to convert words
into making love,
so I became
pliant language of skin
in communication.
We were unrelenting in glossy photos
possessed of narcotics
drugging ourselves
on touch.
You took off your shirt of navy
and threw my linen
on the floor.
We were a fusion of spirit
on the edge of holy breath
in a circle of one mantra
spoken in body.
I let you in where no one has been
to feel the soft places of story
and serenade.
It is not that I think of exploit,
so much as I remember little things
you do not understand.
We were no cartographers of love,
but at least I can say
I knew a rare place among secrets.
I could articulate how rooftops fade,
how watercolor disappears
into tomorrow.

Your baritone voice sounds of ocean
as you slip undertow on the shore of my soul
and I close into a shell
knowing you have run your smooth
hands right into the sanctum
of my bones
but still can't see how
it was slow euthanasia
for me.

Anonymous

In an empty house
we sleep for the first time
to dissolve into sounds no more
than a murmur.

Especially now,
as I walk in our dreams
broken

to see the shadows of uncertainty
curled around one another
in desire.

The link of us
over heaps of sweetness
like a comma
between two bodies
of doubt

that inch closer to one another
and stir the hands
to wake the ghosts of our hearts.

In daylight we disappear
and silent is the sun
as our words land wounded
on the open page.

If I want to visit us
I must return again to the empty house
in darkness
on a street I can no longer
remember.

Except I wrote your name
beside mine
even as we spoke of other things
and I wish now
we had not made ourselves
so anonymous.

Irregular Heart Beats

I am searching the dictionary
for the words to describe how
the world has shifted its axis
since you left.

All I am finding are strange sounds
that cling together by virtue
of their order.

There is nothing to describe
the color of a vanishing heart
or the fragrance of hope.

I remember when you asked
me to wait. I am waiting.

I close the dictionary to light a candle.
The wick burns brightest toward the end.

I close the window. In the street
a saxophone player leans against the wall.
His music reverberates of others
who came before him.

Life is a series of questions:
a parade of irregular heart beats
waiting for love to answer.

Dying Jellyfish Deaths

It is already too late to testify.

I have thrown you back into the sea,
into the silence of color
where language does not reach
and remains unspoken
across distance.

Still in the absence of syntax,
I feel your presence
and know you will arrive again
to land on the shores of my life
naked as a new storm.

Sleep in the Sea Tonight with Me

Sleep in the sea tonight with me
Let's spoon one another completely
It will not matter this talk of death

Sink like a kiss right into my last breath
Where we will have the muse of poetry
Sleep in the sea tonight with me

For you, I will give my body sweetly
And, weep like rain into the sandy depths
It will not matter this talk of death

In a cathedral of hearts we give meekly
As we caress the skin of Love's amends
Sleep in the sea tonight with me

Among ruins, star statues and controversy
Sacrifice your moans to my sutras indefinitely
It will not matter this talk of death

Give your body in prayer as it transcends
In our heavenly waters of haloed mystery
Sleep in the sea tonight with me
It will not matter this talk of death

Drowned Cathedral

At last we are free
from the rock
we had chained our love to.

We swim empty
between there and somewhere

under the transparent sky
no longer bound
by the laments of dying.

We are flesh that is torn
beyond the language of lyrics

past the art of mystery
and into the caves of the heart
as light is turned inside out.

We are the miracle that exists
in ten thousand grains of sand

in the seaweed of saints
and lovers submerged
covered in barnacles.

In a drowned cathedral
we have found each other again
curled in the shell of life.

We Are Stained with Salt

Often when I imagine you
the sea flowers open
and the birds hold their breath
waiting for your arrival.

I would describe myself as shell
worn away by wind, rock and sea,
as mistress of the sands
and the sky is not friendly.

That is the kind of day
when your existence curls out from a wave
better than intoxication, or declarations
of loyalty and light.

I hear your voice as you talk to yourself
of how you would sleep in a church
just to feel the solitude,
not really to believe in God or statues.

But I don't want to think of you
in objects or traversed by lessons
in big dusty places.

I love you more than the holy form
or the permanent mark on the inside
carved by waters and heavy storms.

I have seen how you gather dreams
in your pockets and collect the sea
impregnated with splashes of earth
and the touch of everything.

(*I love your hands*
  fatigued by sorrow and hurt by prophecies.)

So, I make myself an offering
full of emptiness,
wakefulness and stains

waiting on the ground
as it trembles all around us
for the rough comfort
of your embrace.

Eros & the Sea

We start on land with wild pear, bougainvillea,
cisterns, colored pebbles and the cool wind
arm in arm like birdsong and the bell.

It is only this that we want: the murmur
and mint of mystic mornings, the shyness
of the first time that shares the meaning
we seek in the field of hearts.

In this dream we are naked as the sea
and eager to share the same vision
we both remember before the shadows
came to cut us in half.

But we are afraid that we are no more
than bottled ships, stone still
and sealed from the truth of storms.
We play with salutations and saints names
unaware of a tragedy in scene four.

The shore of us is littered with shells
opened in disbelief, blackened seaweed,
and the longing for what leads by hook
and crook to the noetic sensate.

We pretend to be dismayed or surprised
that the sea cannot offer us another expression
of tenderness, that she will not give up
the hostages of flattery or stings of secrets.

Perhaps there is no other choice
when we know death will swallow the last word
on the edge of a wave and peel red starfish
off the rocks of consolations.

Maybe that is why we shut our eyes
to reinvent the ocean full of bluefish,
swordfish, black coral and dolphin.

Maybe we know but cannot help ourselves
when the line is cast, that love

lives in the shrine of simple rituals,
and believes it,
while still fresh in the mouth
and undressing noon.

We know only the oracle of sunflowers,
only the rhythm and taste of mandarin oranges
and that we are weaker than water,
so we say our prayers to sea urchins
and the shrimp of fallen idols.

But knowing all this
doesn't stop us from giving one another
the emblems of pain,
the tassels of love.

It doesn't stop us from kneeling
on the sea floor metallic, deliberate
and begging the mother-of-god
to grant us this love
one more time.

Collector of Seashells

Arrive now with sonnets, prayers
and little earthquakes.

I wish to take nothing from this life
except that I may return to the sea.

When you find me on the shore,
hold me close to your heart, listen
inside the curves and caress me,

then toss me back into the waters
that I may drift into nothingness,
into the bliss of non-existence.

Awakening

From within the ocean of sorrow
a blue light emerges
as the beginning of a love story
which doesn't seek for itself,
keep secrets, or explain
the center of life.

Bone Fragments

A Lost Civilization

Lovers: you and I
not more than an artifact.

What shall I compare it to?

Our hearts are broken,
covered in red sands

as gray birds fly above
in hunt for the truth
or a sign left behind.

How simple it is:

to draw stick figures
in the mold of one
life split in two

leaving others to guess
and measure by the lines
what it is to surmise

from the echo of dirt
and empty sky.

Doubt

He gave me roses
and still I wanted to know
if he really loved me
so, I plucked
one petal off at a time
held them hostage
in heavy interrogation
asking the same questions
over and over again
until all I had left
was the stem of silence.

Dye in the Rock

The weight of our bodies
held us together
painted as a sad fresco
to the end of birthing
and being born.

Finally

the moment arrives
you thought would never come
and it is not:

a homecoming
an understanding
or a kiss.

It is the moment
you realize this is the only time
that ever existed

and it is nothing more
than Jell-O
sliding off a cold plate.

Forsaken

We are barren
not for lack of heaven
but for the absence
of discovery.

Honest Poem

I want to write an honest poem
that reads like a map
directly into an honest city

where I can find you
and tell you I lied that last time.

But all of my poems
are unpaved like dirt roads

and they lead into the back alley
of some shanty town
where closed faces question me.

Knavish

He really did not aim
to fake his religion
or swing on the stars
of borrowed zodiacs.

It was my fault
as the cold sunlight
from his crown of Christ
seduced me like a mirror.

I was an easy mark
as if nothing else mattered
except falling asleep
inside each other.

Little White Prayers

To the third Madonna
*   of our sacred lonely,*

I offer the bleached bones
        of this frail relationship

that choked on itself only because
        swallowing resentment
        never agreed with me
        the way it feeds you

            indefinitely.

Mountain of Silence

She cannot climb the mountain of his silence
or find a cool place to hide
in the barren moments of darkness,
neither in the solitary caves
where the man has etched himself into a wall
no more than a drawing from the past,
starved as a stick figure holding a spear
aimed into a painted future…
where she might wait
for him to emerge from the rocks
colored by pigment and spit;
she might hope for the sun to arrive with a lover
rather than the ghost image of a god.

We are Paleolithic

I find you in a mythical world
half metamorphosed
and tilted in pieces of light.

This cosmic catastrophe:

we cannot return to the sky;
we cannot return to the sea.

Our skeletons are scattered
in the sands and blistered white
from lying in the sun too long.

A small hook of bone:

lost in simple amorphous words
that hope for the impossible.

No Word for this Particular Color

You can't shut out the light,
it will seep into the sides
as a living membrane pressing out
waves and waves
of saving grace.

It won't matter
that someone told you so
or if they were bent backwards
over themselves.

You will know the difference
released in a feverish hush, panting
as it pushes itself out breast bones,
arms and throats.

You can't stop the distant cries,
leaf blowers, hurricanes,
earthquakes and tidal waves
or the maimed hunger
that rises like smoke
up into the skies.

It won't matter
that someone is holding their silence
like an arm full of vodka
or wearing their red hot fear
as a new pair of shoes.

The curtain will still flap around in the wind
and the blinds will bang against the sill
reminding you
that light dances in
through the window.

You can't stop the testimonies
our bodies betray
or the way birthmarks, fingerprints,
and photo IDs tell a limited story
of a new generation afraid
of being stolen.

You will find that if someone
you love is dying
suddenly the light comes in
under everything and bounces off
the ceiling.

Even as you skip through
radio stations listening to waves
of words roll through static,
you will feel the light as it gathers heat,
gathers velocity.

You can't stop
the bare faced racket with cracked lips
from talking too much
or erase the checkered politics
of late.

It doesn't matter
if you had sex, made love,
or found
that it all rises in the morning
with the same after taste.

The waves outside our bodies
still continue to communicate
in frequency,
give off shades
of color.

Either you will believe
that people on the news,
at the market, walking their dogs,
reading magazines,
in stories,
really do love each other,
or you won't.

But you can't stop it.

All at Once

I enter
under the stillness
of dreams
where the secrets
of shambhala
and passions of duende
are hidden from view.

In the end
I fall as a dancer
into the center
of earth
just to hold you
one last time.

Over on Mandala Street

Uproot the Chinese poets we buried in the yard
rooted as wild bamboo and open the secret box
of Shaolin to reveal their perfect sorrows locked
in folded petals and add seeds of starting over
beside the cornerstone of my four mistakes.

Painting the Rain

When I found you solemn
and stacked up alone in an barren room,
I questioned your beliefs.

We seemed safe from storms
because I had no idea how a cloud grew
from one dab of paint.

You said: *"The path of rain is greedy,*
it will always find a way in, just like love,
and after awhile it saturates life."

Earth separated us from the sky,
so you went off for a smoke to contemplate
a God who forsakes his own.

I tossed the palette you gave me
for a bare moment that fell from a star
and arrived half naked.

Palimpsest

Overripe are thoughts that slip down
walls of myth and mind.

Our experiences scatter like ants,
burst in fallopian tubes as cysts.

Who or what is contrived on parchment
to render our feelings of deja vu?

When for all we know, we are mad
in our innumerable dreams that fall...

ephemeral as all our yesterdays
faded and measured by a second hand.

Razor Thin

Love me to death:
I imagine myself bigger than this
self injury, injured self.

Do not ask if I have a higher power
right now, I want to fit
into the shape of my face.

This is my life
stale with metaphor and morning funerals
where not even a prayer

drunk on viridian air of creation
can shake my childhood
of paper clip tattoos.

All I want is to be thin -
thin as a piece of paper
so someone will say, "*She's pretty*"

I wish to believe them
irreplaceable as miracles, smart as Plato
and deliberate as a syndrome.

Tell me once more
how to swim back into the core
of a "happy place."

Then give me air for food,
smoke for blood. It's all I want:
this loving to death.

Solitary

In the gallery of the heart
the moon is always female
holding tomorrow's secrets
more than cool reason
or the plea for companions.

Sometimes angels arrive early
with lanterns of morning
and the celebrity of a rose.

But the memory of elsewhere,
of some other time, draws us
to the center by the brevity
of a love poorly translated
as the lonely verse of a lover.

Faith

I don't want to forget your name.
Yet, easy as the new wind
the first syllable billows into air
lost in the repetition
of water.

Already I wish to fly
on the single sound of you
that escapes me
before it dives into a hush
and sinks in the sea
of our ruins.

Salt in the Heartland

Africa

Your children cannot weep
as their hearts
are swallowed by stones.

The moon has turned red
with shame
and the sky is woeful.

Your sister earth quivers
in absence of peace
and rivers flow in sorrow.

Who will stop this cruel
massacre of pain
and let the stones cry out?

"Night Commuters"

for the children in Uganda

Someone said on the news radio
that they caught the rebel
who forced us to kill our families
and wander in the night.

But we know the limits of survival
and forgiveness, so tonight
we will walk in darkness bare foot,
covered with rags.

Don't ask if we want to go home
because there is no home
just the smell of gasoline
and rust of blood in the mouth.

They may threaten to nail our tongues
to boards or cut them out
but we will not tell all or even a little
of the madness we have witnessed.

The truth is not reserved for the dead.
We have seen freedom chopped into pieces
and the color of life as it seeps
from a dying mother's face.

Our hearts have been carved open and left
quivering in an open field for vultures,
so we walk with bare feet until they bleed
and the world opens their doors.

Seize

the passion again
to burn in my soul
for I have survived

by luck

without the use
of who I wanted to be.

Bone is a Cruel Color

She is raped

while her mother watches
without recourse.

They slice her face...

her father has no choice
but to witness the claw
and scrape of flesh.

On the floor

with my legs crossed
I am reading a poem
for her honor.

    The lines blur

        and blood drains

     from the page.

Free Us From the Claws of Cruelty

Oh visitor, can you help us now? How goes Zimbabwe?
How is the Mother of Africa when the world is watching –
do they not understand our fate is interwoven?

What you see in my country is only the beginning
as Great Death is sweeping the land in famine
after many lifetimes of blood shed in the name of men,
in the name of prophecies, presidents and money.

Do not be mistaken. I was not born for the seed of loss
to be planted in my stomach as a gnawing hunger.
I was not born to watch my family die.

My song was given from the heavens
and nurtured in the circle of earth.

Even if they destroy my totem: brotherhood of man
and I cannot find them or hear their voices,
even if my family is dead...

I know their song. I will sing it.
I will enfold their soul in my arms,
so they will not forget the truth of who we are.

Look into my eyes.

You will find more than sorrow or emptiness.
You will find mercy and the great Zambezi

as it flows from the origin of mankind
from the cradle of civilization...

as it rises in my bones
from the roots of legends, Zulu's,
and a rain making queen.

Walk with me into the heritage of ruins,
through gateways built by ancient tribes,
and listen as they speak on the dry wind
with incantations.

Oh, Great Spirits, this is a land of ancestors
where once women ruled as queens and lovers
and the white lion was free.

So, tell me how it is that our own torture us -
take children for slaves, turn blood against blood,
burn farms, deprive of us care
and leave us with nothing except bare skin
for clothes and eyes picked clean
by humans, by vultures?

I was born to remind you of the depths
to which brutality can drop, just how far
one man can measure another man's life.

I was created from the dust of stars, from many lives,
many spirits living in the waters of Victoria Falls
(before she was conquered, before she had that name,
she was "*The Smoke that Thunders*" by our ancestors).

In my land I serve to warn you,
we are the art disappearing,

so we carve our faces into serpentine
curve around the feet or raise our hands in praise
because after so many lifetimes, regardless of the pain,

all life is sacred.

Except you might not be listening
as our ancestor's die, as the animals collapse,
as men line their pockets with cash.

What happened to balance and tolerance -
to sharing and cohabitation for all?

Will our Mother land go on being filled with
children of rage and brothers that betray brothers?
Do they forget in blindness they were born just as I
for justice and life?

I am the soul that inhabits all souls.
I emerge from the roots of Africa.

Do you hear me? I am not meant for this humiliation.
For the heap of stones and trash my countrymen
have created now of home.

I smell the embers year after year.
I am told the world is watching,
they are coming to help.

When are they arriving?

This is not an expedition or a mission.
I am a child, a woman.
I am the dying and the living.
I have a voice.

I am made of flesh like your flesh.
I too was created from a universe of love,
born in goodwill, in the name of peace
and I deserve to speak –

I deserve to eat.

Red Madonna

Sullen as the desert sands
birdlike as a penny-whistle

she becomes a woman:

blood for gold
as a daughter is exchanged
for cows, traded for coins.

Cattle killing is epidemic
as cutting cunts
then sewing them up
to bleed again

from the burning heart,
from the womb of loneliness.

One hundred ninety-five nights
scarlet is translated in spades
listening to a half moon
in the cage of his manhood

she prays for rain.

Sleepwalking in Africa

Flush and slender is your back
imported and pressed to my breast
in the nightmare heat
as I unfurl from the sheets
to tip toe across the reptile floor
listening to baboons cough
in the mindless dark of dark
it is as episodic as your love,
loss, leaving, gone
down a long hole of silence
in a flash of single numbers
on a digital clock that is stuck.
The water from the tap drips
and my dry throat is parched
so I cannot call out for you.
I feel the trail along the wall,
a pattern of death I am familiar with,
pausing I finger a stolen mask
carved from elephant bone.
I remember how they weep for their dead,
wrinkled and gray where you sleep
my eyes adjust to the question mark:
the ghost heap of your body in sheets.
I crawl back in
and feel the salt stick to my legs
hear the hyena laugh
between my shoulder blades.
I close my eyes
to imagine the faces our bones make.

Mazungue

Some say you are a white African
but under the skin you are blue
as a note that sailed from Portugal
to Angola then on to Jersey
where even in the snow the music
of Africa is water in your soul.

When the sun returns melting
all that is frozen and bruised within,
she will bring the orange of blossom
bright as the heart of a desert flute
to play a song of friendship for you
so you will remember who you are.

Mercifully Hollow

Origami figure of bird in prayer
to speak of lakes, cicadas and nothing,
except pain now closed in a casket
that shut your eyes of sky…

reflected in the defenseless morning
where I settle for symmetry
but not lack of touch.

I do not hope for you to return
or the other hundred emissaries for love
or the other thousand champions of valentine.

Finally, someone must bend their shoulders,
know when to drop that last fist of dust;
know where time begins then take a walk.

Leave clutches and nets; leave moonshine;
leave smoke rolls; leave the memories
and fall into a sentence that never ends...

fall into a grave on a humid day
as they put love deep into the damp earth.
I remember you said, *"Never forsake
the kindness of a stranger…*

or the rustle of air in sunlight
when it touches us unaware
and simply disappears.

Osha's Prayer

She wears the bone
of ancient power
hanging on a strap
around her neck -
brown and burnished
by a African sun
this piece of spirit
no bigger than a pill
and cut into a heart aching
for something more
than magic.

The Two Faces of a Wife

She said in Swahili, Shona and Zulu
that she did not want him anymore
but she continued to weave a basket
for his laundry and pour Rooibos tea
in the clay cup. And, he did not drink
her boiled water because she had not
said if the leaves were to cure or kill.

Madonna of the Sun

In the desert of your heart
lives a secret
only the gods have heard
you whisper
in the haze of clove
and gravity -
through the sound
of jasper stones
now worn with carnelian
in hope
of resurrection.

Used

The good news about what arrives second hand
is you don't have to be too careful with it. It isn't
precious. It doesn't mind if you sit on it, stain it
with jam and glue. It isn't perfect and it won't care
that you are not. It doesn't ask a lot of questions.
It isn't interested in knowing if you are right or wrong.
It won't tell you when to sleep or where to shave. It
isn't concerned with being honored in a song; it
doesn't need to be ironed, hung up or worn with a tie.
It may have been traditional or religious once. It may
have spoken several languages; learned numbers
by heart but it won't care if you are a story someone
forgot to write or a lost star. It won't keep you too
long or ask you to be in the mood. You can be half
baked, half smoked, half there. It may have had
manners and been worth gold but it won't mind if you
fall in without a kiss or dream of secrets that remain
unspoken. It won't care if you are retro, vintage
and used. It sees in your face the halo of moments
that give you joy and it is content to let you shine.

I am SHE

I am the red throne of Kali, the orange flames of Sekhmet. The dancing diva of Durga come to call your spirit back into your body Rise up your tired bones to move, sway, rock in the halls of perception.

I am here in the ceremony of removing obstacles from the caves of memory. I am Vulture Crone, Maat. I am the midwife birthing you into ferocious truth, progressive intuition and powerful right action.

I am the lioness licking salt from the salted state of your flesh in the wounds you need to heal. I am here as your sixth sense…as the doorway of discovery to awaken you to the journey you came here for; to awaken you to universal balance.

I am the High Priestess, Luna of the moon. I am Nephthys.

I am the open gateway to submarine gardens. Listen to the secrets of the butterfly starfish and embrace all people: embrace your sister, your children, your ex's and step families too. I am here to encourage you to make amends and let go permanently the grievances you hold.

I am the wisdom of Sophia, the strength of Athena, the gates of hell.

You are the shape shifting vertigo of bodies, of many life times. You are the migration of millions. You are the sorrow of the seas, the sands of change, the receptacle of all life and the willingness to do it again. I am here inside of the image you have of yourself.

94

Look closely:

I am Radha, Laksmi, Hathor, Isis, Venus and Mary Magdelaine.

I am the elements of absolute love that rise up from your hips and speak from the heart of truth. This is not the idolatry of self, neither the desecration of self. You are not here to cherish the false but to awaken beyond the illusion you previously chased and sacrificed for.

I am the mother of heaven, the flowing inspiration of Sarasvati.

I am come to you as the whispering winds of change, as living chaos, summoning the fates, summoning your destiny to rise up and greet you in the mirror every morning. Rise up and know yourself by heart. Ask the stranger you have become to be a stranger no more. Express the love you have hidden, free the hostage of yourself in the unseen, unheard, captive in un-fulfillment. Welcome yourself home.

Honor the love you feel. I am She. I am you. You are me. Love yourself. Embrace me.

Faded Hieroglyphs

There are eternal images in the street
somewhere I have been in my dreams.

I long to return to the sands where lions roam,
sit as sun statues, and roar in the night winds.

I have heard them singing of golden rings,
of fire in my belly, while ashes and petals
blew in the alleys with yesterday's news.

Red with ceremony was the light
and women's bodies did not harden
as they stood in the shadows
watching the winos commune with jackals
and the children play with paper sails.

Among the kohl eyes and black draped women
shopping in the bizarre,

I long to wander free as a winged creature
in the shape of a hieroglyph,
in the shape of mystery,
in the curve of linen.

I long to see the women in the streets
who speak to me from their eyes;
hear them as they say:

Welcome home my sister, my brother.

I feel their presence now
and know that we are one.

If this life is fragile
and we are often too easily broken,
then let today be the day we celebrate love,
so beautifully transparent
with its perfumes and melancholy vines.

Come me with where the lions roam free
and give over your weary heart to rest in mine.

I long to be once again in ancient sands,
in pristine gardens, in God's country
listening to the wild things speak.

Let us be where the journey is loving
and the tribesmen know secrets we have forgotten.

Come with me now
    where the white lions are walking...

  I have heard them
            calling your name.

Our Lady of Dreams:
The Black Madonna

Love is her point of entry
between a pomegranate seed
and a curve

where it slices the heart
hammers two halves into one
then flattens it out again
juiced to the bone, in need
of confessions and weeping.

Our Lady of the Broken

But no one dares to complain
since the Black Virgin's heavy body
is not ascending to heaven
is not wearing the adornments of bliss
but burning with persistence
and reminds the bleeding of uncertainty
and the need for it.

Our Lady of the Un-manifest

She does not utter plentitudes from her blackness,
and from the pools of her eyes,
marked by mystery, are no visions of color
or streaks of luminescence;
no need for what has already happened
or might not ever be.

Our Mother of Consumption and Remorse

Her darkness is a stranger
someone might meet on a side road
by mere happen chance, by accident,
while looking for little misshapen grains;
searching for spices and skulls,
and those rare precious things

as small gestures between two people
unfamiliar with one another
but craving a mystical day of union
like water and open mouths.

Our Lady of Roots and Seeds

Pleasure is concealed behind her face
so nothing can be seen of her meeting with God,
except the Divine child destined for a crown of thorns.
And, since the Enlightenment failed
everyone is on a journey into the abyss of Self -
chanting silent prayers and burning on altars.

Our Mother of Beautiful Losers
Our Mother of the Damned and Confused
Our Mother of the Emptiness and Inevitable Change
Our Mother of Compassion

She docs not have a single name
that is uttered in daylight or covered sweetly
because no one understand her origins
and only the naked walk with her in the flames.

We sometimes call her The Void...

Our Lady of a Dark Star
Our Lady of Skeletons
Our Lady of Caves

without a stained glass window
or a litany of Sunday's unholy afternoons,
neither a rose in the belly of the soul.

Our Mother of All Things

She gives birth to an untidy universe
peels the robes of an unknown mistress

as Love forcefully enters
with a loud crack that scars and chants
that seduce, ravage, swallow, and devour.

Our Lady of the Mysteries

enshrined in the caves of our hearts
to consume us wholly submerged
in this subconscious dying to ourselves
in Love eternally.

Hope

Tattoo it inside my heart
like someone's name
scratched on prison walls.

Sky Rivers

Ablutions

I need you like the rain
to fall into the shrine
of my chest where my heart
sits in flames, burning
from too much of this
world, too much of this
pain, burning with desire
to feel the flowers
of love bloom again.

Amnesty at Daybreak

Rise up from a dead sea
to give the dust of stars their praise
and answer the night with a soft voice
as she sheds silence.

Listen as the cicadas leave their shells
and the flowers stretch
into the epoch of dawn
as new lovers.

Let the entire world greet you
with their open arms
in faded light and kisses
from fallen stars.

Let Us Speak the Language of Love

How shall I tell you what I see in you, that your infinite beauty, your infinite glow shines above all other things in life waiting? Do you know that I hold the secrets of my love for you inside, when I can feel that nothing in me has died, nothing is forgotten? When I can feel that you have already gone, already left, become distant and remote.

How shall I tell you the truth of who you are when you have lost your will, gone deaf to reason? When you have cut your hair, given up your jewels, forsaken the treasures of our journey? Can you see that this self-inflicted torture is pain for us all?

By rounds of song with praise in devotional solitude, I sing, I write of a dream where the light of love remains full of hope, full of each other, overflowing, pouring life into that which has yet to be born. My love for you burns bright as a lantern even in the cold, in the rain, across the map in a world too full of turmoil to notice the last sweet smile on your lips before sleep, as the meadows darken and the taverns open.

Do you see how this light of majesty illuminating from the galaxy of your soul falls upon my face as I wait for the moments that bring you closer to my lips? Let yourself rise again from defeat with your arms open. Stand in grace and give your sweet nectar of love freely. I have seen the flowers open for your smile. I have seen the monarchs kiss you and angels sing for you.

I beckon now for your heavy heart to be healed and for aching betrayals to be washed clean. Do you think no one has heard your cries in the night? If they could not it is only because they were overcome with crying their own tears.

Let your face be free of revenge, free of grudges embedded like stones under the eyes or a mouth trailed by frowns. I have seen your face luminous, wet with tears, crying with laughter and joy and kissed by love and kissed by betrayal again and again.

I long to see trust in your eyes. How shall I convince you that the world needs your love sailing across the sky as a wish? Needs you to be pure and true as a gift that goes on emanating light forever, needs you as I do?

Born from Heaven

for Natori & Auguste

I plucked you out of a star field
gave my salt water body to you
and let you enter me.

Cupping you as a small shell
skull attached to a mere tail
spooling around love's finger.

I held you where water is mute
where it is shallow contained,
but full of life.

And, you slumbered as a ship tossing
in movements of daily murmurs,
listening to notes of my heart.

Consoling yourself in smallness
with a little foot not knowing itself
or the ordinary people waiting

to meet you, now drunk on flowers
their throats parched from singing,
from contemplating your face.

After you arrived we envied your lips
crowned you nocturne and we loved
kissing your nose.

So, you see how you must survive
fights, the municipal and harsh;
those who chisel at the sun?

Because I carried your light in me
even before we agreed to share
this cup of body.

Why I am Not Afraid of the Dark

I.

I offer thanks to the darkness
dressed in a mean spectacle
of cruel mysticism.

For without the black hearts,
there are no flowers of light.

II.

In praise of Mapplethorpe's lilies
and celebrations of impotence
choked around scrotums
and confirmations
of barbed wire.

He would not turn away from
pierced language
of borrowed debauchery
and circumstance.

III.

The black hole of a face
pretends to suck infinity,
propagate the myth
of madness.

Let them have a thin smile
of satisfaction -

It is hip to be a victim
and practiced in the art
of disturbing.

IV.

When this cacophony
of the overly anxious
dies down...

it is the carnival of the sun
with sweet perfume
and solar flares,

not the trivia of slide shows,
that burns heaviness
from the mind.

V.

Angels appear -
turn shadows inside out.

And, who knows what
is reflected by the rays
bounced off darkness

in smooth radiance,
like some beauty
that cannot be captured?

VI.

In a vortex where hearts join
and eclipse one another
through portents of mystery,

darkness is a canvas
for brilliance and prisms
that favor stars.

I offer thanks to the light -
listen as the heavens open
and worm holes cry out.

Keeper of the Stars

He found them in her eyes
kissed them from her lips
and scoped them off her breasts,
torso, hips, and legs…
put them back into the sky,
one by one
so they would fall
into her laughter
and he could collect them again.

No Such Thing as "I" in the Universe

Well, not exactly.

In the beginning
I peer into the heart
of the Sun.

You roll it
in the palm of your hand
as a glass stone;
not white, but red
and gold.

You point to the bright spot:
there is a hole
in the sky
and the sun is so thirsty
it drinks our skin.

But nobody takes it seriously
this idea we are born
from the stars.

I need the fire myth
of lion colored solar flares,
disturbing the uncommitted,
as much as you do.

Let the fire
burn straight into me,
magnetic in the naked
daylight.

We are sure of nothing
and hope for everything
together in the gallery
of the sun.

You won't say why,
except your religion is the cosmos,
and language echoes incandescent.

So, we vanish
into the ultraviolet eye of love
and embrace the sky.

The Sun is Just a Star

If we rationalize it,
there will be no end to our excuses.

It is heliocentric (a revolution in Ptolemy's grave)

    Luckily, fear of mockery talks in epicycles
    that shiver in the light,

so no one dares to say the unspoken words:

Earth is not the center -
    is not even a star.

        She is transient: copulating
        with war, bloated with wages;
        hot with reasons for love
        and preludes to lift skirts;
        she is redolent with rejection,
        flowers and tarantulas.

But we cannot blame her for all that vanished
or for the dethronement of God
and acid rain or the fat bellied cartoons
that children swallow like pop tarts
and sugared genocide.

Anyway, it is the Sun's fault:

    without financial responsibility
or holy duty
living off the skin of innocence

        (*how exquisite he is*)

    scathing us with drunken words -
happy to give autographs,
and burn in the charity
of blind praise.

Rain Madonna

A crushed star is crying
in her final hour of beauty
as she shakes the clouds
to wet her children
with promises of a love sutra
in gentle rhythm.

Some Angels Wear Blue

After 100 nights of listening to your pain
they cover themselves in your sorrow:
stitch by stitch as they weave the color
melancholy from your bruised shadows.

Sun bells ring in a bird shaped silence
to remind you that the heart will sing.

In the morning you will find the two
halves of you have been sewn together
by delicate hands who filled the spaces
with stars cut from the ovals of your tears.

I Believe in Your Broken Wings

A restless bird is your soul
waiting to enter the house of eternity
to be reborn as a blue lotus -
as enlightened.

And, I believe in you
in spite of the blood, mud and straw.

If you collapse
to the thunder of threatening sky
sideways blowing of rain
then you will forget
your purpose is to carry
heaven to earth.

Your humble body
translates the sorrow of trees
as you lie in the valley of broken wings
where a thousand things join.

In silent sacrifice
you have given your love
to the barefoot, to the crowns,
and to those with power,

while taking nothing for yourself
except the quiet learning of gratitude
and generosity.

As you enter the house of truth
to open the windows...

leave the land of burnt flesh

forsake countless exhaled breaths
leave terrors of brooding nights
forsake teeth, meat and bones.

Let peace be unfastened
from the streets of heaven.

I have witnessed your long journey
between stars. I have seen the earth shape
a story under the weight of feet
as the seeker is forever walking
with love stuck in the throat.

Come into daylight without end
where the face of evil is erased
where kindness lives side by side.

Yes, I too have fallen face down
only to stand again in awareness
to discover

there is nothing beyond
the idea of self, nothing
except Love.

Yes, you are blessed.

It is past time for you rise up
to release the dust of sleep...

claim your birthright out of chaos,
resurrect the temple of your heart.

You Are Loved

When you are in pain
and those cowards
think they know all
there is to know
about you…

listen to your heart.

She will tell you
the real story of Love
and all of those cowards
will just run out the backdoor,
while you will remember
with a smile that

Love is all there is,
and most importantly
that you are loved too.

122

By Now the Light Has Faded

The holy rage has gone down
with the sun of anger
and the story of enlightenment
is writing your name
through a sliver of moon,
so in this moment of reflection
the ashes of burnt hearts
are carried by the wind
to settle in the deep waters
of the unborn.

About the Author:

Zayra Yves grew up in the San Francisco Bay Area in the early 1970's, listening to the Beat Poets at City Lights and evangelical preachers on Sundays. She has traveled extensively on pilgrimages to sacred sites around the world and continues to find new ways of expressing the art. She is an independent artist who has produced and released two audio poetry collections: *Crowned Compassion; Sleep in the Sea Tonight with Me*. She is published in numerous print journals and on-line magazines: *The Zimbabwe Situation; The Panhandler Quarterly; Voices for Africa; Eyes of the Poet; Kreativ; Reflections IIT Madras (India); Edge Life Magazine; Poetry Life & Times*; *Astropoetica* and *Alehouse Press*. She has appeared as a featured guest on the West Marin Community Radio for "House of the Poet" and on SW Radio Africa's "Outside Looking In," as well as many other radio stations and on-line audio programs. Her audio poetry collection *Crowned Compassion* has appeared on *Integral Naked, TWiN, Perfectly Said, Mazungue Studio One, Zimvibes and Coolfire*. Currently she lives in Northern California with her family.

www.ingramcontent.com/pod-product-compliance
Lightning Source LLC
LaVergne TN
LVHW091154080426
835509LV00006B/683